MW00767867

. . . LIFELINES . . .

Making Wise Life Choices

...LIFELINES...

MAKING WISE
LIFE CHOICES

JOHN TRENT

Tyndale House Publishers, Inc.
WHEATON, ILLINOIS

Published in association with the literary agency of Alive Communications, Inc., 7680 Goddard Street, Suite 200, Colorado Springs, CO 80920

Library of Congress Cataloging-in-Publication Data

Trent, John T.
  Making wise life choices / John Trent.
     p. cm.—(Life Lines)
  ISBN 0-8423-6021-2 (sc)
  1. Christian life. I. Title. II. Series.
BV4501.3 .T74 2003
248.4—dc21   2002152205

Printed in the United States of America

07 06 05 04 03
6   5   4   3   2   1

. . . ABOUT LIFE LINES . . .

The Life Lines series is designed for *real* people in *real life* situations. Written by published authors who are experts in their field, each book covers a different topic and includes:

- information you need, in a quick and easy-to-read format
- practical advice and encouragement from someone who's been there
- "life support"—hands-on tips to give you immediate help for the problems you're facing
- "healthy habits"—long-term strategies that will enrich your life
- inspiring Bible verses
- lists of additional resources—books, Web sites, videos, and seminars to keep you headed on the right path

Life Lines is a joint effort from Marriage Alive International and Smalley Relationship Center. Marriage Alive founders and directors David and Claudia Arp serve as general editors.

Whether you need assistance for an everyday situation, a life transition, or a crisis period, or you're just looking for a friend to come alongside you, Life Lines offers wise, compassionate counsel from someone who can help. This series will connect with you, inspire you, and give you tools that will change your life—for the better!

Titles in the series:
Life Lines: Connecting with Your Husband—Gary Smalley
Life Lines: Connecting with Your Wife—Barbara Rosberg

*To Marty Kertesz,
our outstanding office manager
at StrongFamilies.com.
Thank you, Marty, for the wisdom
and wise choices you've shown
in managing our ministry.*

John and Cindy Trent

. . . CONTENTS . . .

In Search of a Guide

Should I end my marriage?
  Is it right to sign the form that says, "No medical heroics"?
  Should we send our child to Christian or public school?
  Why did my father leave my mother?

In a single week in my counseling practice, these are the kinds of questions raised. And each person who voices these questions has a life story as unique as his or her fingerprints. But although the individual circumstances are different, each person is searching for the same thing: wisdom.

And they're just like us. Aren't we all faced with big decisions that require wisdom? Hardly a week goes by—sometimes hardly a day goes by—that we don't feel as if we've been chosen to "come on down" during a TV game show. There's an important decision placed before us: Will it be the curtain or the box? The clock is ticking and the crowd is yelling at us with their advice. How will we stay calm? Whose advice should we take?

You may have picked up this book because you're facing a potentially life-altering decision—just like those four people who came into my practice that week asked those four questions. Perhaps, like the first woman, you're wondering if you have an escape clause from a difficult marriage.

It could be that you're caught on the horns of a different type of moral or spiritual dilemma—like the pro-life advocate who spent years championing the lives of the unborn. Now she was emotionally racked over a life-and-death decision concerning her own dying father. Should she sign the "no medical heroics" form (meaning no feeding tube for her semicomatose, suffering father), or would that be giving up on life? Would that be dishonoring to God?

> **When faced with challenges . . . we need more than a map. We want a guide!**

Still others are somehow trying to push back the curtain that covers the future, or they're trying to come to grips with something from their past. I've heard the same anguish from the couple who wanted so much to make the "right" decision for their third grader (whether to put him in Christian or public school) as from the man in his midfifties who still struggles over why his father *really* left the family when he was only eight.

When faced with challenges like these, it's easy to feel like folks from a one-stoplight town who are visiting a huge city for the first time. We need a lot more than a map shoved into our hands and encouragement to go it on our own. We want a guide! We want someone to walk beside us down the narrow streets—amid

. . .

all the strangers. We want someone who can interpret mysterious road signs and help us navigate eight-lane traffic circles on our way to the safety of our hotel.

THE VOICE OF WISDOM

Fortunately, there is such a guide for challenging problems like those listed above as well as for the unique issues in your life. She's actively applying for a job. She shouts from the street corners, beckoning each of us to put her to work. Here's what it says in God's message to the world, the Bible:

> Listen as wisdom calls out! Hear as under-
> standing raises her voice! She stands on the
> hilltop and at the crossroads. At the entrance
> to the city, at the city gates, she cries aloud.
> (Proverbs 8:1-3)

Wisdom is repeatedly personified as a woman in the book of Proverbs. That's certainly by design. Wisdom isn't pictured as a testosterone-loaded taxi driver. It doesn't ignore us and drive by as we wave, or finally stop and shove us helplessly into the backseat and race us to an unknown destination. Wisdom is pictured as a woman who uses truthful, caring words—words that call, guide, encourage, and direct us as we learn to "walk in wisdom." Her words are an extension

. . .

of the counsel offered by God, the author of wisdom himself, who also offers to be our Guide.

> For such is God, our God forever and ever; He will guide us until death. (Psalm 48:14, NASB)

For those who will take off the world's noisy headphones for a moment and pay attention to wisdom's call, the benefits can be staggering. God says, "Choose my instruction rather than silver, and knowledge over pure gold" (Proverbs 8:10). Like selling all your tech stocks a month before the fall, a wise decision can bring an absolutely priceless level of peace and rest and calm to your busy, stressed-out life. (Just ask anyone who has made a poor decision and paid steep emotional, physical, or financial costs.)

HEARING THE CALL

I'm going to assume that you're at least a little like me—that you're interested in finding God's wisdom to face a certain issue or situation. Perhaps it was the title of this book or the back-cover copy that caught your eye. Even if your spouse is making you read this book, or you're not fully convinced that God has something to say to your situation, I hope you'll read on.

Wise decision making has become increasingly difficult in our "Little House on the Freeway" world, partly because the sheer number of important decisions we face continues to multiply. It can be discouraging at times, but don't give up! God has given us many principles to guide and help us if we'll only take the time to discover them.

Where do we begin, then, to find the wisdom we need, the wisdom that God says is clamoring for our attention? We'll start by taking a look at why it's so tough to make good choices. What barriers do we need to overcome, and how can we do that? Next we'll look at Life Support—immediate, tangible help for making good decisions.

Finally, I'll tell you about some healthy habits that will help you respond wisely to some common challenges we face. If you put these into practice, you'll find yourself conquering problems like anger, fear, and procrastination, plus improving your relationships with others.

I'm convinced that God, the author of all wisdom, wants to share that wisdom with us. Stick with me as we first take a look at some of the challenges standing in our way.

THE DECISION DILEMMA: THE CHALLENGE OF MAKING WISE CHOICES

If you've ever watched a national or Olympic diving event, you've heard the television sports commentators use the three words *degree of difficulty*. In the opening round, divers can choose to do a swan dive or a simple back flip. But with each successive round comes the expectation of an increased degree of difficulty. Soon it's not just a swan dive that keeps you in the competition but a double back layout, pike position. And forget a front flip if you want to be successful—we're talking triples without a splash.

DECISIONS, DECISIONS!

You may not care much about diving, but you're living in a world where the degree of difficulty for making wise decisions is already at the "medal round" and steadily going up. The sheer number of choices we face is exploding like never before.

For example, couples in 1950 had few options, outside of adoption, if they couldn't conceive. Today the choices are many. With new drug therapies (for the husband or wife), in vitro fertilization, surrogate parents, and foreign adoption, today's childless couples have numerous options. I even once read a newspaper headline that screamed, "Web Site Offers Supermodel Eggs." Yet couples will need more wisdom than ever in facing so many of these uncharted choices. And it's not just the exploding number of choices set before us. There has also been a steady erosion of clear guidelines to help us make wise decisions.

WHEN GUIDELINES ARE GONE

Years ago, there was a young man named Johnny who had tremendous talent in the swimming pool. He swam for the Chicago Athletic Club and was setting national age-group records consistently in his home pool. Yet whenever Johnny competed in an "away" meet, his time would plummet and he'd rarely even place.

Then one day his coach recognized the problem.

. . .

The pool at the Chicago Athletic Club was one of the first in the country to have large black lines painted on the bottom of the pool to mark the center of each lane. At away meets, the pools had no such lines. When he could see those clearly marked lanes, Johnny was unbeatable. But send him out in the "real world" of unmarked lanes, and he kept falling behind.

That is, until his coach finally recognized the problem. "Johnny!" he roared. "You aren't swimming straight! You don't have that black guideline, so you're wobbling all over the pool!" Slamming his hat down on a kickboard at one end of the pool, he sent Johnny to the other. "All right," he ordered. "That hat is your goal. Fix it in your mind, draw a mental line to it, and swim for it."

There is a standard for right and wrong and a source of wisdom to know it.

Which is just what Johnny Weissmuller did on his way to winning twenty-four national and five Olympic gold medals—all before becoming "Tarzan" in the movies.

In our quest for wise decision making, the degree of difficulty is compounded by the lack of moral or spiritual guidelines in our world today. Our great-grandparents used to call Sunday "the Holy Sabbath." Our grandfathers called it "the Sabbath." Our parents referred to it simply as "Sunday." These days, we lump it together with that other day off and call it "the weekend." From the American Civil Liberties Union to situational ethics to a culture that considers any belief in moral or ethical absolutes as intolerant or ignorant, there are no more lines on the bottom of the pool to guide us.

What's more, any lines that once were a part of our national conscience have been scrubbed off by a court system that has banned prayer in public schools and fought to allow distribution of condoms in high schools. Any hint of right and wrong has been sandblasted off the bottom of the pool by special-interest groups who don't want any behavior to be labeled sinful or immoral (even if it clearly exploits or harms women, children, the elderly, or the unborn).

In the original language of the New Testament, the word *righteousness* literally means "to stay within the lines." These days, no one is really sure where the lines are or who was supposed to draw them. But in a world with no lines, how can we make right choices? There is a standard for right and wrong and a source of wisdom to know it. Each person will have to find his or her own lines—and hang on tight to them.

LIVING IN VIRTUAL REALITY

In addition to the explosion of choices and the lack of moral, spiritual, and societal guidelines, there's a third factor that makes decision making so difficult. Many people today are opting for "virtual reality" over objective reality. In this Internet Age we live in, the way we connect with humanity is increasingly through a flat screen rather than face-to-face. That lack of personal contact can absolutely confound wise choices.

Do you know how many incoming college freshmen meet new friends? That's right—it's the Internet. Rather than meeting real people for the first time in the dining hall or the student center, they meet an "Internet profile" that's often sanitized or inflated (or both). And it's not just students who are moving away from face-to-face interaction.

The Pew Internet and American Life Project reported that more than 55 million Americans go online each day, and more than a third of them spend at least an hour on the Internet. Some 15 percent of those daily users spend more than three hours a day on-line.[1] And where does one find this time in his day? Norman Nie, director of an "Internet and Society" study done at Stanford University, concluded it came at the expense of time spent with family and friends. "We're fast moving to a world where interaction takes place at a distance," Nie says.[2]

How does this at-a-distance connecting affect wise decision making? Read the following description from a short story by E. M. Forster called "The Machine Stops":

Imagine, if you can, a small room, hexagonal in shape, like the cell of a bee. It is lighted neither by window nor by lamp, yet it is filled with a soft radiance. There are no apertures for ventilation, yet the air is fresh. There are no musical instruments, and yet, . . . this room is throbbing with melodious sounds. An arm-chair is in the centre . . . and in the arm-chair there sits a swaddled lump of flesh—a woman, about five feet high, with a face as white as a fungus. It is to her that the little room belongs.[3]

People in Forster's world communicate with each other by looking into a round, glowing, blue plate in which they see each others' faces. When they want books, music, or food, they press a button and the machine delivers those things instantly. They rarely see people face-to-face. They spend their time instead attending lectures with other users of the machine from around the globe. And, perhaps most important of all, there are no new ideas being talked about or shared. All thoughts are fourth-, fifth-, or even tenthhand, passed down from original sources long forgotten and unquestioned by all.

Sounds like a pretty accurate picture of life in the Internet Age, right? But did I forget to mention that

. . .

E. M. Forster's story was written in 1909? It was supposed to picture life hundreds of years in the future. Yet his chilling look at people's dependence on staring into the "blue plate" has become reality in less than a hundred years!

Effects of isolation

Wise decision making today requires face-to-face contact with loved ones and mentors and close friends. Dealing with issues may require time with a trusted counselor or people who have "been there." Yet while we have the technology to be more "connected" to people than ever before (computers and Palm Pilots and cell phones and wireless e-mail), most of us are more isolated and lonely than ever before! Poet and critic T. S. Eliot captured the problem well: "Television is a medium of entertainment which permits millions of people to listen to the same joke at the same time and yet remain lonesome."

We need real people to interact with if we're to build strong relationships, which we'll see is an essential element of making wise decisions. Isolation doesn't bring truth and wisdom. Connecting with a flat computer screen as your main source of insight fails to provide subtle distinctions or important, full discussions.

Our diagnosis so far has focused on three external challenges to wise decision making:

- The exploding number of decisions we must make
- The lack of moral or spiritual guidelines in our society
- The increasing isolation in our Internet Age

But before we turn to timeless biblical solutions, let's look at some obstacles we may face. These "misbeliefs" and internal challenges can block, confuse, or even cripple our response to wisdom's call.

... 2 ...

LEAPING THE HURDLES THAT HOLD YOU BACK

Recently I spent a few incredibly frustrating hours trying and failing to get on-line. I went through all the various menu items, read the troubleshooting section in the user's manual, reinstalled software, made sure the modem was plugged in, everything. Everything, that is, except checking to see if the modem's phone cord was plugged into the wall behind the desk. (I won't mention which daughter had been behind the desk, unplugged the cord from the wall, and forgotten to plug it back in . . . nor the lecture she received!)

I had every expectation of getting on-line, but that required a live connection, not just good intentions. I see a similar problem in people struggling to make wise choices. The desire to gain God's wisdom is un-questionably there. Yet it's like the phone cord is un-plugged at one end.

Over the years, I've seen four circumstances that can consistently leave people feeling like they're "unplugged" when it comes to connecting with God's wisdom:

- They've come from a background full of poor choices
- They're first-generation Christians
- It seems like their choices really don't matter
- Wisdom's choice seems to come at too steep a price

A DOUBTFUL INHERITANCE

Let's face it. Not all of us came from homes where wis-dom was woven into the daily fabric of our life. I think most of us would love to have grown up in George Bailey's family in *It's a Wonderful Life,* but, unfortu-nately, too many of us grew up down the street in homes more like *Nightmare on Elm Street*!

Coming from a long line of poor choosers can create a strong internal pull to replicate what we've seen, heard, and experienced. In the Bible, that's referred to as "the sin of the fathers" being passed down from generation to generation (Exodus 34:7, NIV). It's the pull to do the wrong thing we've seen modeled in the past instead of choosing to do the wise or right thing today. It might tempt us to say things like:

- "They got away with cheating on their taxes. Why shouldn't I?"
- "Nobody I know bothered to say, 'I'm sorry.' What's the big deal?"
- "Go with your gut. It's a waste of time to pray or ask for help."

For some people, watching a parent, sibling, or spouse make poor choices can pull the plug on their own decisions to do what's right. Yet growing up in a home where poor choices were modeled doesn't have to unplug your ability to link with God's wisdom. Coming from a single-parent, non-Christian home, I'll be the first to admit it takes courage to confront a poor past. But you can take the high ground and reverse the hurtful negative patterns. In fact, just by taking the first steps toward facing and overcoming those generational "sins of the fathers," you may find you have something in common with some of our nation's greatest heroes.

Taking the challenge

One of the most heroic exploits of World War II involved the Second Ranger Battalion scaling the cliffs at Pointe du Hoc, France. Their mission on D-Day morning was to take the cliffs and destroy the 155-millimeter cannons looking down on Omaha Beach. If those gun batteries had raked their deadly fire down on the beach, they could have wiped out many more soldiers and even threatened troop ships offshore. Since the Allies were unable to deliver a knockout blow by air bombardment, it was up to the Rangers to accomplish this "impossible" task in a mission now immortalized in the national D-Day Memorial in Bedford, Virginia.

> **Our God generously, openhandedly, without judgment or scorn, is ready to give us his wisdom when we ask.**

Using cannon-propelled grappling hooks and huge iron ladders, the Rangers fought their way to the top of the cliff. Yet when they finally reached the gun emplacements, the big guns weren't there! The gun mounts remained, but the Germans had moved the guns to protect them from the air bombardment and weren't able to reinstall them before the Rangers arrived. The cannons were later found in an apple orchard and destroyed with grenades.

What does this heroic episode have to do with making wise decisions today? The Rangers' heroism in completing this seemingly impossible mission can be a tremendous example for people from difficult backgrounds. For those of us who came from broken or

. . .

non-Christian homes, the past can loom up as imposing as the cliffs at Pointe du Hoc. Yet if we'll face up to the task, asking almighty God for the strength to keep moving toward his high calling, we'll often find the victory is in the climbing.

What's more, many times the terrible fear or threat that has so worried our minds and memories ends up being an empty one when challenged. Take my wife, Cindy, and me, for example.

I came from a single-parent home where my father walked away from our family when I was only two months old. My wife, Cindy, grew up with alcoholic parents in a home filled with outbursts of anger at unpredictable times. Neither one of us came from a Christian home or anything close to it. And if the truth be known, we both harbored fears about whether we'd be able to move past our history of broken relationships to build a lasting, loving home of our own. Those fears weren't unfounded. Indeed, if someone were to take an "aerial view" of our ability to make a solid, lifelong commitment based on our backgrounds before we were married, the task would have looked as challenging as those Normandy cliffs. But through prayer and careful choices, Cindy and I have created a strong and lasting marriage.

That's the way past problems and history can look:

huge and scary and invincible. They can sap our courage, block any efforts to get past historical barriers, and even drain away hope that things could be different for us.

Fear binds us to yesterday. Choosing wisdom links us with the doable today.

Breaking from the past

It takes courage to walk out-of-step with your past. It's a challenge that can look as high as D-Day's cliffs or even Mount Everest. Yet listen to the words of the first person to reach Everest's summit. When asked about his accomplishment, Sir Edmund Hillary said, "It is not the mountain we conquer, but ourselves."

Think about the wisdom in Hillary's statement for a moment. Most of us would see the mountain as the obstacle. He saw rightly, just like the Rangers or someone committed to breaking from the past, that the biggest challenge lies within.

The cliffs and mountains we face can be scaled one step at a time. Or to see it a different way, the poet Robert Frost wisely observed, "The best way out is always through."

The best way to get to the top and beyond a challenge is by facing the issues and going through them. At the time of this writing, my precious wife and I have been married twenty-two years—she from an al-

• • •

coholic home and I from a broken home. Over those decades we've struggled just like any other couple, but we've also discovered an important truth: The fear of ending up just like our backgrounds can be faced and backed down.

Each time we've chosen the solid footing of wise decisions, it has dealt a blow to our backgrounds. And each year that has passed, we've gained even more confidence that God's wisdom is for anyone who asks—not just for a privileged few. For example, it's not just for those who come from a long line of Christians.

FIRST-GENERATION CHRISTIANS

I'll never forget standing in a prayer group of Promise Keeper speakers several years ago before we were to speak to a stadium full of men in Boulder, Colorado. As we stood in a circle, held hands, and prayed, I felt totally unworthy to be in that group of godly leaders. In the circle was Bishop Porter, who at that time was pastor of a dynamic inner-city church. He represented the third generation of pastors in his family. Dr. James Dobson also stood in that group. On his father's tombstone are carved the words *He prayed*—a testimony to his father's incredible commitment to prayer and his unwavering faith.

However, as I stood in that circle, I couldn't call on

a history of faith. As a first-generation Christian, I could understand comedian George Gobel's famous line, "The whole world is a tuxedo and I'm a brown pair of shoes."

When it was my time to speak, I began by telling my own story. Then I asked each man who, like me, had grown up in a non-Christian, single-parent home to please stand to his feet. And while you couldn't literally count, clearly more than half the stadium—some 25,000 men—stood up.

Wisdom—guaranteed to those who ask

Many first-generation Christians can feel as if spiritual wisdom is beyond them or simply out of their reach. After all, they never had a father to pray with them over decisions or a mother to lead in daily devotions. Yet that afternoon, as I prayed with those third- and even fourth-generation Christians—and later stood with the thousands of first-generation Christians just like me—a single verse kept coming back to my mind: "If you need wisdom—if you want to know what God wants you to do—ask him, and he will gladly tell you" (James 1:5).

Our God generously, openhandedly, without judgment or scorn, is ready to give us his wisdom when we ask. When you go before God, asking for his wisdom, you'll never hear the words, "You should have known that!" or "How could you not even know the basics?" Nor will you hear the kinds of things an impatient teacher or an uncaring boss might say in answer to your coming to him or her: "Take it up with someone else," or "I'll tell you, but it'll cost you," or "I can't believe you're asking that," or "What a stupid thing to ask." What you'll gain instead each and every time you go to your heavenly Father is a willing, listening ear from the one "who gives generously to all without finding fault" (James 1:5, NIV).

Coming from a difficult background or its common corollary, being first-generation Christians, doesn't disqualify us from gaining God's wisdom. In fact, in some cases it might even give us greater humility to ask and seek—and find.

On matters large and small, go to God for wisdom. Corrie ten Boom, the noted Holocaust survivor, puts it this way: "Any concern too small to be turned into a prayer is too small to be made into a burden."

Yet for some people there's a third issue that can seem to unplug us from God's wisdom. That's the nagging voice in our situational-ethics world that tells us the choices we make really don't matter.

DO YOUR CHOICES REALLY MATTER?
Does God really care whether you pick tan or cream carpet?

. . .

Is the God who hung the stars really interested in what school you attend?

Does it really matter what person you marry?

Will God even notice if you leave the security of your current job to take that position with a start-up?

What about placing your child in day care so you can earn extra money for the down payment on a house?

The very title and topic of this book implies there is indeed a caring, living, breathing, personal God who is interested in the details of your life—which include the choices and decisions you make. Now, this isn't to say that we should pray, "God, do I take a right or a left to get to the store?" There's a whole range of general knowledge and thought that lies outside the search for God's wisdom on numerous daily-life issues. But the same God who knows when a sparrow falls and numbers the hairs on your head is indeed concerned with the choices that burden your heart and life.

What's more, seeking wisdom from God implies that there *is* a path to follow. Put in the words of Scripture, "I will teach you wisdom's ways and lead you in straight paths" (Proverbs 4:11). His promise is to lead you, not on an unmarked trail that only expert trackers have to scramble to find, but along a clear—if narrow and less-traveled—pathway that leads to peace and rest and life.

. . .

Following wisdom, not feelings

Unfortunately, the idea that a living God can and does have a "way of wisdom" for us to follow is scoffed at by many today or, at best, tolerated like a child's crayon art. In our world, the idea of a biblically based way of gaining wisdom is outdated or even labeled as dangerous.

The idea of a divine or biblically laid-out path is far too exclusive for many to believe. And it's particularly difficult to swallow for people looking for approval of a lifestyle they know lies outside that biblical path. In large part, that's why entire special-interest groups have insisted that all paths and all choices are equally right and have bullied adults and children for decades with this "socially correct" view.

For example, a classic moral dilemma first presented to public schoolchildren in the 1960s was to talk about three people adrift in a lifeboat with a serious problem. While there are three people in the boat, there is only enough food and water for two. Different variations of this situational-ethics dilemma involved some combination of either an elderly person or a doctor or a celebrity or a child in the boat. Students were then asked to decide how to solve this problem—which most interpreted as meaning they had to choose which person should be pushed out so the others could live.

. . .

According to those doing the teaching, the right answer to this moral dilemma was . . . there wasn't a right answer! In short, what they were teaching was that it was each student's choice who lived and who died because all right and wrong boiled down to the situation, not to any biblical absolute such as the sanctity of human life or the intrinsic value of each person. Students were encouraged to go with their feelings, not some external set of rules or ancient "commandments."

Accepting absolutes

What happens when a generation of children grows up being told that the choices they make are independent from any absolutes—that there is no divine "way of wisdom" to follow? To see the very worst result, just look at the Columbine killers and bomber Timothy McVeigh. These young people lived out the words, "There is a path before each person that seems right, but it ends in death" (Proverbs 14:12).

No wonder Timothy McVeigh chose the poster poem of the 1960s, "Invictus," as his final words.

> *Out of the night that covers me,*
> *Black as the Pit from pole to pole,*
> *I thank whatever gods may be*
> *For my unconquerable soul.*

. . .

Strapped to the death-row gurney, he stared defiantly at the witnesses and relatives of the victims he'd sentenced to death in the Oklahoma City bombing. No remorse. No sorrow for the loss of innocent life. Just the same cold cruelty of the Columbine killers, who said "Peekaboo" to a girl hiding under a table and then shot her dead. Witnesses described the hatred in McVeigh's eyes—a clear picture of his last words and his educationally and socially endorsed attitude:

> *I am the master of my fate;*
> *I am the captain of my soul.*[4]

After all, if there is no God who lays out a right road, then all roads are equally right or wrong. Indeed, if there is no way of wisdom and life, then the ultimate, horrible end is for people to conclude that they have the right to decide who's to live and who's to die. People who fear that accepting God's Word as their life standard is too exclusive are excluding themselves from genuine peace and rest.

Search all you want; there are no words of hope or rest or peace or love in the "Invictus" poem. But hope and rest and peace and love are all promised by the God who created you himself; they are the result of seeking and applying his wisdom.

The truth is that there is a way of wisdom. God does care which road we take and what decisions we make, large and small. And if we'll follow his way, we're told, "Fear of the Lord gives life, security, and protection from harm" (Proverbs 19:23).

WHEN WISDOM COSTS TOO MUCH

I have a good friend who likes to say, "You'll never lose weight as long as there are éclairs in your refrigerator." In other words, you can have great intentions of losing weight, but leaving chocolate-covered temptation within arm's reach is a way of signaling defeat before you've lost a single pound.

Something similar happens if you say you're searching for God's wisdom on a subject, but inwardly you're reserving your final answer for yourself. You want to know God's will and wisdom before you make a decision, but you aren't ready to make all your decisions according to that way of wisdom. That's having the words without the sacrifice—like this young woman whose story is far too common:

She grew up in a Christian home. In high school, she made a personal commitment, giving her life to Christ. In college, she worked at a Christian camp where she recommitted her life and talents to God. She even helped lead a Young Life club, sharing Christ with hurting kids and teaching young women. But that was all before she met an attractive young man who actively avoided anything to do with Christ or her faith—the same young man who asked her to marry him a year later.

Because I was acquainted with the family, this couple came to my office to see if I would officiate at their wedding. We talked about their relationship and life goals, and I'll never forget his saying to me, "She can believe that God stuff if she wants. But that's not me. I don't believe any of it." I thanked him for his honesty and had to tell them that I couldn't perform their wedding ceremony.

You see, it's clear in God's Word that believers are not to be linked with unbelievers in close, interdependent situations like marriage. Such hard wisdom can sound restrictive and perhaps even vindictive to a couple that's in love—as it certainly did that day. How un-Christian to say no to something they felt was so right. But oil and water don't mix, no matter how often or how loudly we insist that they should.

This young man's contempt for what his fiancée believed meant she would have to become two people each day. She could try to be a person of faith when her husband wasn't around, but then she'd have to shut the door on her faith to try to please him and keep the peace.

It didn't take them long to find someone else to do

the ceremony. And while their marriage lasted six years, major issues began to surface within weeks of their wedding. After she spent six years disconnecting herself daily from her faith, her husband announced he was moving in with another woman, leaving this young woman with their two precious children. He made that decision with no remorse and no concern for the tears of the children or the consequences to his wife. As the captain of his own soul, why shouldn't he? And of course, in the meantime, his wife had cut herself off from her family, friends, and faith and had a net "zero" in the life-support-systems category.

Making the tough choices

I've seen that tragic story replicated hundreds of times over the years. Each time it begins with people who concluded—at the front end of their decision—that the initial cost of following God's clear wisdom on a subject was just too steep. But the hidden costs of walking away from wisdom multiply the pain people think they're avoiding—often multiplying it many times over.

I can't promise that as you turn the page and learn more about finding God's wisdom in various life areas, you'll always like what you find. But learning more clearly what it means to "walk in wisdom" will, in the

. . .

long run, lead you to untroubled sleep, freedom from fear, and fullness of life all your days.

To summarize, so far we've seen that

- We're facing more choices than ever before.
- Strong moral and spiritual guidelines are no longer a part of our culture.
- We're becoming more disconnected from others at a time when we need them more.
- The initial cost of choosing wisdom can sometimes seem way too steep.

But we've also mentioned that God's wisdom isn't hidden from those with a difficult past, nor is it reserved only for those from families of faith. We've acknowledged that our choices, large and small, do matter to almighty God. And we've taken the long view to see that the way of wisdom, though sometimes costing greatly at the front end, pays off in lifelong dividends.

Now we'll turn our attention to defining wisdom— and coming up with some tangible ways we can make decisions that are in line with God's wisdom.

... 3 ...

LIFE SUPPORT: SMART STRATEGIES
FOR MAKING CHOICES

Wisdom is certainly a word that consistently pops up in books or in conversation. But just because a word is familiar to the ear doesn't mean we really understand its meaning. To make sure you get the picture of what wisdom means in biblical terms (and in your search for God's wisdom), let's look at an example.

Let's say you wake up one morning and walk out to get the paper. As you bend to pick up the paper and stand up, you think your eyes must be playing tricks on you. Your car, which you waxed the afternoon before and parked right in front of your house, has been totaled!

■ ■ ■

The bad news is . . . during the night a hit-and-run driver has put you on foot!

The good news is . . . you have excellent car insurance. You'll be able to replace your car with another of equal value (even adjusted for inflation).

But there's more bad news. While you have insurance, in order for your coverage to apply, you have to pick a replacement in the following way:

- No test drive.
- No opening the doors or looking under the hood.
- No reading auto-magazine reviews or talking to owners.
- No asking hard questions like, "Would you happen to have the name of the 'little old lady' who was the only driver of this car?"
- And most of all, absolutely no setting two different cars you like side by side to examine their various merits.

"No way!" you might say. You'd never buy a car under those conditions. Which, by the way, would be wise. The last stipulation in particular is a literal picture of what the biblical word *wisdom* means. In Hebrew, the language of the Old Testament, words often picture a literal object. For example, the word picture behind the word *anger* in Hebrew is literally "flaring nostrils." The word picture for *blessing* is literally "to bow the knee." And the literal picture for the word *fear* is "kidneys" . . . for reasons best left unexplained.

What's the word picture behind the word *wisdom*? It's the act of setting two things apart—of putting distance between like things in order to see the obvious or subtle contrasts. Can you see the wisdom embedded in such a picture?

WEIGHING THE OPTIONS

To go back to our car example, let's say you narrowed your search to two vehicles. Setting each model side by side and comparing the various pros and cons—at least on paper, if you couldn't actually get the two vehicles in the same place at the same time—would indeed be a wise way to make a decision.

In the Bible, you don't see the example of picking a car, but you are presented with the picture of a jury trial that illustrates the wisdom in setting things apart. Proverbs 18:17 says, "Any story sounds true until someone sets the record straight."

In a trial, hearing only one side of the story isn't enough to make a wise decision. Wisdom involves examining both sides in order to make a fair ruling. Laying the opposing viewpoints side by side in order to see the actual merits of the case is crucial to justice being served.

· · ·

This can help us better understand what we're praying for when we ask God to grant us wisdom. Namely, we're asking him to highlight the differences between choices set before us. We're asking him to help us honestly consider which choice is most reflective of his will. We're asking to lay our will next to his will and Word—and to have the strength to choose what he would choose.

But setting important decisions aside to examine their merits closely is a rare option in an emotionally driven world that wants to decide everything right now! In fact, I can remember a time when one fool made a very unwise decision, spontaneously and based squarely on emotion instead of fact. The decision cost him dearly. It's a familiar story because that fool was me!

SEPARATING FACT FROM FICTION

Before Cindy and I were married, she had worked very hard as an elementary-school teacher. After we were married, she continued to teach until Kari, our oldest child, was born. In those seven years before children, she expended tremendous effort in training and encouraging her students. During that time, she also put several thousand dollars into her teacher retirement account.

When Cindy left teaching, we had a decision to

make regarding her retirement fund. At least, it *should* have been a decision. Instead, the decision became a slam dunk after I sat down a single time with a new friend from church. This person had been an FBI agent for twenty years. Now he'd retired from public service to become a financial planner. Or at least, he was in the process of becoming a financial planner.

In process or not, he seemed to know far more about investments than I did. In fact, over breakfast, he shared with me a limited-time, "can't miss" opportunity for a very few extremely discerning people. It was an offer that seemed perfect for Cindy and me! All we had to do was put in a little . . . and rake in a lot. It was safe, full of upside potential, and had no downside risk even worth discussing.

Just hearing there was "no risk worth discussing" should have made me run away from the table! But unfortunately, I kept munching my toast. When he finished with his pitch, did I kick the tires on his offer? Did I look under the hood by reading the fine print in his proposal? And especially—like the very word *wisdom* suggests—did I set his offer side by side with another investment option and evaluate the merits of each?

I wish!

Forget wise decision making. I was too busy

buttering a second order of rye toast, picturing how this investment would butter our bread in retirement. All I could think of was the beach house we could live in during the winter and that mountain chalet in the summer. As you might imagine, I went straight home from our meeting to tell Cindy about how lucky we were to be among the select few to participate in this amazing, limited-time opportunity. In fact, I convinced her to invest her entire teacher savings into the "limited gas and oil" partnership our friend was offering.

> Seeking wisdom will indeed slow down our choices, even as it shores up our defenses against making emotional or often costly impulse decisions.

I remember assuring her that morning that this investment simply couldn't miss. Then, two years later, I remember spending many nights trying to explain to her why we'd lost every cent of her hard-earned money. (There was that slight "risk" part I missed in the fine print that stated that hitting only empty holes could mean losing all your investment.)

Before I go any further, I need to say I've only done something that foolish with our finances one time in twenty-two years of marriage! For one thing, I like sleeping indoors. For another, after that experience, I've taken to heart what the word *wisdom* means in Scripture.

. . .

MEASURING AGAINST A STANDARD

To separate fact from emotion or, in this case, fact
from fiction, is a key to finding wisdom. To pull apart
the pieces of a decision and lay them next to a com-
peting standard is indeed helpful. To lay the decision
next to God's unchanging Word is even better.

For example, let's go back to the young woman in
the previous chapter who chose to marry the *GQ*
model look-alike—the young man who was the dedicated non-Christian. What if she had brought that decision before God and truly looked at both sides of
what she was deciding? What if she had laid God's
Word (and listened to her parents' and close friends'
repeated warnings) on one side and her feelings of
love on the other, and she had judged each honestly?

"That's hard to do!" you might say, which is absolutely true. As you'll see in the "life choice" areas that
follow, searching for God's wisdom calls for us to use
those "little gray cells" that Agatha Christie's fic-
tional detective Hercule Poirot uses to solve cases.
Seeking wisdom will indeed slow down our choices,
even as it shores up our defenses against making
emotional or often costly impulse decisions.

In order to further illustrate this idea of laying an
important decision side by side with another, let me
give you a tool I use in my counseling practice. I've
titled it a "Seeking Wisdom Worksheet," and it's a

way for an individual or couple to lay an issue or decision alongside a contrasting choice.

I'll use a real-life example first, and then we've provided a blank "Seeking Wisdom Worksheet" for you to use on a decision or issue you're facing. Our real-life example involves a married couple. The husband was happily employed in the D.C. Beltway, and they were living in a beautiful home in Maryland. That's when the husband was approached about an exciting new job offer with a start-up company in Arizona. Here, included with permission, is the actual "Wisdom Worksheet" they used to talk through, pray about, and consider this major life change. I've edited it a little for length; each column had more statements than we had room to print.

You'll see their "Wisdom Worksheet" is divided in half. At the top of one side of the page is the word **Positives**; on the other, **Negatives**. Each of these two sections is further broken down into an A and a B section, creating four equal-width columns on the page.

The Positives section is where you record the "pros" of each side of the decision. In this example, the positives of making the move to Arizona are represented by the A column. The positives of staying in Maryland are represented in the B column.

Then there is the Negatives section. Here you'd write down as many "cons" as you can think of for

POSITIVES		NEGATIVES	
A: If we choose... to move to Phoenix	B: If we choose... to stay in Maryland	A: If we choose... to move to Phoenix	B: If we choose... to stay in Maryland
• Chance for job advancement • Better winter weather • Chance to share Christ with parents* • Know of good churches • Best college friends moved to Phoenix • Feel like job is done where we are • Slower pace of life*	• Job security • Love our house • Close friends • Four seasons • Kids can stay in schools they like	• Hot summers! • Have to find new doctor and dentist # • Have to sell our house to buy a house in Phoenix • Kids will have to make new friends	• Give up "advancement" potential • Is our job really secure? • Kids won't really get to know their grandparents*
Key verses to consider: *"Be strong and courageous! Do not be afraid or discouraged. For the Lord your God is with you wherever you go."* JOSHUA 1:9			

each aspect of the decision. Again, A represents moving to Arizona, and B represents staying in Maryland.

LAYING OUT THE PROS AND CONS

Beginning with the initial mind-set of "the more thoughts the better," the couple started writing down as many pros and cons on each side of the decision as they could. Then, after this free flow of thoughts and feelings, they went back and looked more closely at each of their responses.

Each comment, positive or negative, that seemed upon closer evaluation to be very short-term in nature received a # next to it. For example, you'll see a # next to "Have to find a new doctor and dentist" in the

"Negatives-A" column. While finding a new family physician would indeed be a potential negative if they moved, it seemed to be a short-term concern as they talked about it further. The Arizona company was offering excellent health benefits with the ability to choose their own primary-care physician from the top hospital in the state.

Then they went through their list of positive and negative comments, placing an * next to any items that seemed to bear directly on their quality of family or spiritual life. For example, "Chance to share Christ with parents" would be an example that held clear spiritual implications and received an * mark. The comment "Slower pace of life" was given an * as a decision affecting quality of family life.

Finally, at the very bottom of the sheet came a section titled, "Key verses to consider." Obviously, there are no verses they could find that specifically said, "Thou shalt (or shalt not) move to Arizona." (Although I did see a road sign once in Oregon that said, "Thanks for visiting but thou shalt go back to California.") Here the couple listed any verses that God had laid on their hearts during their discussions or prayer times. You'll see they put Joshua 1:9 on their sheet. This was written by the husband, who tended to be less of a "risk taker" than his wife. In spite of his hesitation at giving up a secure position, he felt that

POSITIVES		NEGATIVES	
A: If we choose...	B: If we choose...	A: If we choose...	B: If we choose...
Key verses to consider:			

Joshua's encouragement to "be strong and coura-
geous. . . . For the Lord your God is with you wherever
you go" was something they should consider.

While laying out the pros and cons, evaluating
them more closely with the (#) or (*) designations,
and listing any pertinent verses didn't make the decision for this couple, it certainly helped. It also helped
increase their communication about possible fears
and concerns, and it helped them to clarify their
wishes and goals. In short, the very act of taking time
to search out God's wisdom in this decision brought
them closer to God and to each other—and it gave
them confidence when they made their final decision.

. . .

I've included a blank "Wisdom Worksheet" for you to copy (with permission given for this page only) and use on a decision you might be facing.

Understanding the word picture behind the word *wisdom* and having this "Wisdom Worksheet" can help you as you search for God's wisdom. Before I turn to additional thoughts about gaining wisdom in seven common "life choice" areas, there's another aspect of the search for wisdom that's important to highlight.

TWO FOR ONE

There's actually a kind of "two for one" offer when you go after God's wisdom, because any search for wisdom will lead you to its fraternal twin—truth.

While I haven't always been a fan of the late Ann Landers's advice, I thought her feedback to one very egotistical person was excellent. Her advice to someone writing under the name "Mr. Pride" was, "Know yourself. Don't accept your dog's admiration as conclusive evidence that you are wonderful."

I'm all for people having a good self-concept, but Ann Landers was right in this case. Your dog's reaction to your coming home may not give you a true picture of how you're doing as a person. (Particularly if the dog is anything like Cracker, our eighteen-year-old "Terry-Cocker-Poodle-not-to-mention-lots-of-other-things-we're-not-sure-of" mix. She always does

. . .

the same full-body, touching-an-electrified-fence shaking thing when she first sees you, whether you've just come in from a weeklong trip or a trip to take out the trash.)

One of the greatest benefits of seeking wisdom is that it forces you to traffic in the truth. You won't find wisdom if you're lying to yourself or others. And truth is a priceless gift in our day and age, when people would much rather feel good about themselves than face the fact that their dog may be wrong.

At the highest levels of government, professional "image managers" spin the truth and base major decisions on polling data, not on principles or biblical standards. With truth so corrupted at the top, the trickle-down effect to the average person results in only trace elements of truth at street level. But a tremendous benefit of searching for God's wisdom is that it requires you to "walk in the truth" even as God walks in the truth. It gives you a true north by which to align your life. But how do you know the truth amidst all the confusion?

STICKING TO THE TRUTH

The answer is as timeless as God's Word. King David wrote, "All your words are true; all your just laws will stand forever" (Psalm 119:160). Jesus himself repeats this truth, asking of the Father on behalf of his disciples, "Make them pure and holy by teaching them your words of truth" (John 17:17).

Wisdom and truth always share the same path. Find one, and you'll find the other. Follow one or the other, and either one will lead you to the words of Scripture. And if you will follow God's unchanging Word when it comes to your decisions, you'll find it's like stumbling upon a beautiful mountain lake. Countless trees, all postcard-pretty, line the hills around a lake so still and clear it reflects the nearby mountain all the way to its peak. This is the kind of forgotten place in our "fly over" world that was once overstocked with trophy fish but hasn't been fished in years. Now it's just waiting for you to cast your faith upon the water. And when you do—*Wham!*—it's like catching two fish on one hook (which is possible—I've done it!). Wisdom and truth—both keepers—are both trophy mounts in a world full of empty promises and confusing talk.

Wisdom and truth—what a two-for-one deal! Begin your pursuit right now. There is wisdom available for all the decisions you'll face today—and tomorrow, whether they're big or small. In the chapters ahead, we'll hit a few of the more common life choices— maybe one of them is one you're facing right now. The overall healthy habit of pursuing God's wisdom will be our guideline.

RUNNING TO WIN: PURSUING GOD'S WISDOM

Have you ever looked in the mirror and said, "It's time to develop some healthy habits"? That's exactly what I did after going to a high school reunion party. I was having a great time seeing people I hadn't seen in decades and introducing them to my wife, Cindy. Then the program began and the master of ceremonies started the program by saying, "It's great to see everyone here. There's Jeff Trent (my twin brother) looking like he could still play football. And there's John looking like he just swallowed a football!"

Ouch! Later that evening, as I looked with sadness at my reflection in the mirror, I made a momentous, "I'm going to get back to regulation size" decision. My brother, Jeff, had kept in shape running marathons. If he could do it, then I would too. No more "Mr. Football" jokes for this guy! I'd have one last piece of cake . . . okay, maybe two more . . . just to make myself feel better after being slammed in front of all those people I hadn't seen in years, and then I'd get on my way to getting back in shape.

I picked a marathon that was almost a year away, trained faithfully, and finally the day of the big race came. What an experience!

STARTING STRONG

It was early on a Sunday morning, and San Diego was wrapped in clouds—something the southern Californians call "June gloom" but which all the runners deemed a blessing. When I stepped into the #9 Corral, there were just six minutes left before the starting gun sounded—I'd overslept and almost missed the start! So much for prerace jitters. Assigned bib number 9592, I was the bologna in the sandwich. There were literally ten thousand people in front of me and ten thousand people behind me!

Up ahead (meaning way up ahead) were the elite runners—superhumans who would run the 26.2 miles at an average 5 minutes, 26 seconds per mile! Behind these world-class athletes came the real-world runners. Twenty-one corrals full of 21,000 optimistic,

. . .

"I'm going to get my T-shirt!" runners just like me. All of us were confident we would rock the Rock 'n Roll Marathon.

How'd I do?

I started well. I had great form as I ran past the ESPN II cameras focused on the starting line. (Of course, the cameras weren't actually broadcasting when I passed the starting line, but they were there!) Two-thirds of the race was no problem. I even stopped at the twenty-mile mark and grabbed a pay phone next to one of the water stations. I quickly called collect to Cindy and the girls back home in Arizona, shocking them and giving them the news, "I'm doing great!" Brimming with confidence, I thanked them for their prayers and energetically stated, "Just six more miles to go!" That's when the course started climbing uphill—and my race time started going downhill.

As I jogged up a series of short but steep hills starting around the twenty-one-mile mark (for an Arizona boy used to training in the pancake-flat desert, picture the Rockies or Andes), I began to notice something new. Suddenly I was passing the vast majority of people around me instead of the reverse. Most people were wisely walking up the steep part, especially since the sun had come out. They planned to start running again when things flattened out. But on each of these short, steep hills I ignored the walkers and acted like Rocky in the dramatic stair-climbing scene in *Rocky I*.

The course finally did flatten out the last three miles, but by then my legs (and my pride) had been deflated as well. It was then that the lady with the jogging stroller passed me. And as if that wasn't bad enough, a guy with no shirt, who definitely needed to put on a shirt, plodded past me as well.

But I didn't give up.

I didn't sprint the last mile like I'd rehearsed in my mind a hundred times. My finish was more like the scene from *Chariots of Fire* where the runners are in slow motion. But like the lazy Mississippi, I finally flowed across the finish line at the Marine Corps Training Depot. My foot-blistering time was lit up above me . . . 5 hours and 21 minutes. I almost nipped the winning runner from Kenya who finished a mere two hours and forty minutes ahead of me.

Even though I had finished in 10,431st place, the many helpers at the finish line still acted excited, wrapped me in a cool-looking, silver, space-age blanket, and slipped a really cool medal over my head. I still had enough energy left to grab a banana, thank

> The best part of running a marathon has nothing to do with the race itself. It's the habits formed in the weeks and months before race day that seem to count the most.

. . .

God for getting me through all 26.2 miles, and be thankful for all those who had prayed I'd make it "Alive in 5." At least I'd finished; there were 5,100 who started that day who didn't make it. And of course, afterward, there were the inevitable reflective moments on what I'd just done.

CROSSING THE FINISH LINE

I share my marathon experience with you because it holds so many parallels to real life. Not the blisters and body odor but the way life seems to have that group of elite runners way out in front who breeze through life's ups and downs. Then there's the optimism and eagerness of so many of us who want to do something well and cross the finish line with our hands held high. But there are also those steep hills that come way too late in the race. They pose the kind of trial that can quickly turn pride into humility. When you watch other runners disappear ahead of you, you start wondering, "Am I ever going to make it?"

Running a marathon taught me more about Hebrews 12:1: "And let us run with endurance the race that God has set before us." And I certainly viewed Ecclesiastes 9:11 in a new light: "The fastest runner doesn't always win the race." But most of all, I think the lesson God hung around my neck that day didn't involve crossing the finish line at all. I discovered the best part of running a marathon has nothing to do with the race itself. It's the habits formed in the weeks and months before race day that seem to count the most. It's the training, not the 0.5 seconds of national airtime when I made a group shot on television. It's the patterns being set, even more than the genuine simulated-metal medallion at the end.

It's getting up and running when no one is looking. It's struggling through the aches and pains that tempt old legs to quit. It's cutting out the diet colas and bags of chips and welcoming a beautiful new day in prayer as I pound the pavement all by myself.

To paraphrase Jack Nicholson in the Academy Award–winning movie *As Good as It Gets,* it's those habits that "make me want to be a better person."

In case you're thinking of lacing up your shoes for a marathon attempt of your own, the thrill of finishing twenty-six miles lasts about as long as the soreness in your legs. But the healthy habits can change your life. And that's what brings me to the goal of the next few chapters of this book.

As a fellow runner in life's marathon, I'd like to give you some "race tips"—some running advice on healthy decision-making habits. These pointers won't get rid of any extra pounds, but they might help you achieve the day when wisdom's medal can be hung

. . .

around your neck. For life, as the writer of the book of Hebrews tells us, is indeed a race:

> Therefore, since we are surrounded by such a huge crowd of witnesses to the life of faith, let us strip off every weight that slows us down, especially the sin that so easily hinders our progress. And let us run with endurance the race that God has set before us. We do this by keeping our eyes on Jesus, on whom our faith depends from start to finish. (Hebrews 12:1-2)

The wisdom of the following chapters comes right from God's Word, applied by me and others who have put in many more miles than I have while going after God's wisdom and his best. It's my prayer you'll always stay focused on Jesus, who is the "starter" and finisher of our faith, and that you'll always develop and maintain healthy habits like

- running for God, not the cameras,
- praying always,
- picking up the phone to encourage others along the way,
- walking up the hills with friends,
- and never, ever giving up . . . even when the lady with the jogging stroller passes you.

. . . 5 . . .

HEALTHY HABIT #1:
GETTING RID OF ANGER

A few years ago I spoke at a men's retreat in northern Arizona. During the afternoon, the men were given instructions to pick one elective that most closely matched an area in which they were struggling. There were sessions offered on finances, on prayer, on Bible study, and on being a godly businessman. Approximately 40 of the 300 men in attendance went to these workshops. The other 260 showed up at mine, not because I'm such a great speaker but because they were told to pick the topic they most needed help with—and I was speaking on how to deal with anger.

Lots of men and women need wisdom in dealing

with anger. In fact, many of us are like the man who drove his young son to preschool one day. The next day, Mom drove the youngster to school.

"Mommy," the little boy asked as she took him out of his car seat. "Where are all the idiots?"

When the mother asked what he meant, the little boy said, "Daddy drove me to school yesterday, and we saw seven idiots!"

Unfortunately, at times my own kids could echo that young boy's words when it comes to my driving. I've read Proverbs 14:29, which says, "Those who control their anger have great understanding; those with a hasty temper will make mistakes." But somehow, it seems all those bad drivers in front of me are the ones making mistakes—not me, in my totally justified rantings. But if you're serious (and honest) about searching for God's wisdom in your life, then dealing with frustrations—even frustrating drivers—needs to become a godly benchmark in a mature faith. Proverbs 29:11 makes that clear: "A fool gives full vent to anger, but a wise person quietly holds it back."

So how do you gain wisdom when it comes to dealing with anger?

Get a pacifier. Not the $1.29 type meant for infants—even though I have seen adults throwing tantrums as bad as a baby's! The kind of "pacifier" I'm talking about is described in Proverbs 15:18: "A hothead starts fights; a cool-tempered person tries to stop them." How do you "pacify" contention?

ADMIT IT'S NOT YOUR ROAD

Without exaggeration, 220 of the 260 men in my anger workshop admitted having outbursts of anger on the road. They didn't experience road rage to the degree that they got pulled over by the police or parked their car and screamed at someone, but they had that feeling of bubbling-over frustration that too often elicits a rude (or even profane) comment, leaving the men feeling shame, not relief. What's one solution to this common frustration point?

Try taping an index card with four large initials, *INMR*, on your dash. The initials stand for the words *It's not my road*. Our frustration when we drive is often because we've mentally made driving an ownership issue. Those crazy drivers are blocking "my" lane, or slowing down "my" commute, or keeping "me" from hitting the posted speed limit.

> **Make a commitment today that you won't cause "secondhand suffering."**

It's amazing what a simple, silent prayer before you head to work or off on an errand can do for your drive-time frustration level. For a week, try looking at that index card each time you start the car and praying, "God, remind me that it's not my road—but it's my character that I'm revealing when I drive."

For others, I'd suggest getting a Christian book on tape or a sermon series and pushing Play each time you start the car. Then when you hit a traffic snag, say out loud (assuming you're alone), "God, this is great! I get some extra time to learn something outstanding about you from this tape." Instead of steaming in frustrated fury as you sit in traffic, redeem the time as you learn more about your Redeemer!

RECOGNIZE THAT THE OTHER PERSON IS NOT THE ENEMY

Without question, the second area most likely to set off the men in my anger workshop came as they waited at a checkout counter. As a frequent traveler who stands in countless lines, I can certainly relate. Once again, that internal ownership issue seems to surface when we're in line. "It's my time they're wasting. . . . It's ridiculous they don't have qualified checkers. . . . Those people in front of me are asking pointless questions!" Waiting in line can leave some of us feeling like a shaken-up soda bottle by the time we reach the counter.

Here's another anger-management suggestion for those serious about acting wisely. Instead of clenching your teeth as you wait in line to check out, try praying for each person in front of you. That includes the elderly lady who has to set each item slowly . . . carefully . . . on the conveyor belt. What if she were your mother? Would you pray for her then? It even includes the checkout person who is obviously new and can't figure out which key to push. What if that were your son or brother on his first day as a checker?

How different would your attitude be when you finally got to the checker if you'd silently prayed for her up to that point—instead of glaring at her to hurry up because she was ruining your life?

GIVE A SOFT ANSWER

In the "I get so frustrated with my spouse" department, here's another tip. It's something that takes practice, but it's helped tremendously in my home as well as in many others.

Often husbands and wives can be like thermostats. If one person raises his voice or anger level, the other one instantly moves up her emotional thermostat to match. Word for word. Anger for anger. But one way to keep things at a comfortable 72 degrees all year round is to ask a calming question if your loved one comes across a little intensely: "This really is important to you, isn't it?"

For example, when I sense by her words or tone of voice that Cindy is frustrated with me or someone else, my natural inclination is immediately to match her frustration level. For example, if she were to say something like, "You told me you'd fill up my car and you haven't. When are you going to do that?" my natural response might be to hurl back words like: "Look who's talking! You told me you'd have that shirt ready for today and it isn't!"—perhaps spoken in an even stronger tone than hers.

But what if the next time you heard that edge in a loved one's voice, you practiced something unnatural but very wise? An often-quoted verse in the Bible tells us, "A gentle answer turns away wrath" (Proverbs 15:1). When you hear your spouse express a concern with potential "set me off!" emotion, ask him or her softly, without sarcasm, an anger-deflating question. For example, in response to the "Why didn't you fill up my car?" question, respond with a comment like: "I can tell having the car filled up with gas is really important to you. I'm sorry I didn't get to it. I'm doing something right now, but would you like me to stop and follow through on filling up your car instead?"

Asking questions and recognizing that the issue is important to your spouse can be a powerful way to head off dishonoring words. Of course, you may have to pick your spouse up off the ground the first time you express that kind of understanding, but such questions and acknowledgment can go a long way toward keeping the tone at home in the comfort zone.

DON'T PASS IT ON

Several years ago there was a best-selling book called *Contact: The First Three Minutes.* It was a book that insisted that the first three minutes you see a person are hugely important in how you connect with him or her. Now fast-forward to a very frustrating day at work. Let's say you didn't get a third of the things done you absolutely needed to do. Then toss in dozens of crummy drivers on the way home. No wonder you feel justified in letting the first person that comes within range hear all about your frustration. Right? Not if you're wise in dealing with anger.

So often we point our anger at the first target of opportunity. Yet too often that point person ends up being our spouse or one of our children. Make a commitment today that you won't cause "secondhand

---

FIVE WAYS TO DEAL WITH ANGER

1. **Admit it's not your road.** Let go of your sense of ownership.
2. **Recognize that the other person is not the enemy.** Pray for the people who frustrate you.
3. **Give a soft answer.** Don't respond to anger with anger.
4. **Don't pass it on.** Don't unload your anger on the first person you see—often your spouse or kids.
5. **Don't storm the gates.** Recognize that in God's book, keeping your temper makes you a hero.

---

suffering." Think about those first three minutes of a conversation. Like secondhand smoke, blowing off steam can be toxic to your loved one when you first meet him or her after a long day. (In the next "Healthy Habit" on dealing with fear, I'll share a powerful method of dealing with built-up frustrations before you get home—so keep reading!)

DON'T STORM THE GATES

In Proverbs 16:32 we read, "It is better to be patient than powerful; it is better to have self-control than to conquer a city." Can you imagine? Keeping your temper in check ranks you right up there with MacArthur's retaking of the Philippines or Patton's breaking through at Bastogne on Christmas Day! While the comparisons might seem far-fetched, God looks at a person who "rules his spirit" as if he or she were a conquering hero. That's high praise from the King on high!

Each time you choose to remain patient when the traffic light refuses to change, the return call doesn't come, your teenager doesn't want to clean up her room, or the car breaks down, look at it like having a medal pinned on your chest for actions above and beyond the call of duty. In fact, one way to remind yourself of this is to go by the local party store and actually purchase a plastic gold medal.

.   .   .

Hang the gold medal over the rearview mirror of your car, put it on your desk at work, or tape it to the refrigerator at home. Then, act like you're the Colorado football team getting ready to leave their locker room. They all reach up and touch a sign that says, "The best athletes in the world go through these doors."

Whenever you hold your anger in check, reach up and touch that medal, but instead of praising yourself, say, "Thank you, God, for helping me win the battle with my anger this time. I can only do this because of who you are, God, and the power you give me to be my best."

... 6 ...

HEALTHY HABIT #2:
FINDING FREEDOM FROM FEAR

I remember working with one individual who had developed a great fear of being fired by his employer. He had excellent performance reviews, and the company and its industry were thriving, not cutting back. But he was in his midfifties, and somehow the thought of being cut loose from his profession at his age chilled him to the bone. In fact, the fear became a tremendous barrier in his attitude toward work as well as his relationships at home.

How do you break free of those types of mental roadblocks? How about applying more wisdom from God's Word? Or, in this case, try to apply God's Word each time the fear surfaces. Let me explain.

BREAKING FREE FROM FEAR

The next time you're plagued with worry or fear, get out another 3 x 5 card. No initials this time. Instead, you're going to create your own "Stop—Think" card. On one side of the card write a verse that particularly encourages you to confront whatever fear you're facing. Our friend who feared losing his job picked Philippians 4:13: "I can do everything with the help of Christ who gives me the strength I need."

Then sit back and wait for the next time Satan or your own insecurity drives that fear to the forefront of your mind. For this man, it was minutes after he had first written the verse on the card. But this time, instead of lamenting his lack of faith or commanding himself not to think fearful thoughts, he simply pulled out his card. He read the verse he'd written, said a short prayer thanking God for the truth of his Word, and asked him for a peaceful heart. Finally he turned the card over and put a single mark on the back of the card before putting it away.

Each time that specific fear resurfaced, he started the whole process over again. He took out the card, read the verse, prayed, turned the card over, drew a mark, and put it away.

If you try this, don't be surprised if the first day you end up with fifteen or more check marks on the back of your card! But stop to think what fifteen (or more) marks means: You've linked your fear fifteen (or however many) times with God's Word, and you've prayed and asked God for his help and strength more than a dozen times! That's far better than letting fear curl you up in a ball!

The next day, follow the same process, noting as you did on Day One how many times you take out the card. And the next day. Before long, it's very likely that you'll be looking at your "fear" quite differently—and perhaps even be finished with your card. Consistently linking your concern with God's Word and prayer can often disengage fear's paralyzing grip.

In the case of our friend who was worried about being fired, he began talking with his wife about what he could do if he lost his job. Previously, he had been so afraid even of the thought that he couldn't talk about it even with his wife. In this case, it turned out his fear of losing his job didn't materialize, but his faith in a God who could give him strength in the face of fear certainly did.

> **Replacing the fear that trips you up with a clearer focus on almighty God can be a powerful way to add wisdom to your walk of faith.**

Proverbs 29:25 reads, "Fearing people is a dangerous trap, but to trust the Lord means safety." Replacing the fear that trips you up with a clearer focus on almighty God can be a powerful way to add wisdom to your walk of faith.

PROTECTING YOUR HOME FROM FEAR AND ANGER

On most days Diane felt like the second woman referred to in Proverbs 14:1: "A wise woman builds her house; a foolish woman tears hers down with her own hands." In Diane's case, she was coming home from work so frustrated, she'd often storm in and yell at her husband over next to nothing. She even caught herself wanting to shake her young daughter when she did something wrong. The tension was so thick in her home when she walked in from work, her three-year-old would run away when she saw her. That wasn't the kind of home Diane had prayed for and dreamed of while she was growing up.

That's when a friend—a wise police officer who often was exhausted and stressed on his job as well—told her he'd made a change that helped his own young daughter run toward him rather than away. I call the technique "Palms Down/Palms Up."

What the police-officer friend had learned was how to keep that day's dose of anger or fear from walking in the front door with him. Considering his job, you can imagine the kind of difficult issues and words he heard most days. What kept his relationships strong at home—and honoring to God—was the "rest stop" he made a half mile from his house.

Each day this policeman would stop his squad car at a park near his home. (In his city's police department, the officers drive their cars home as a neighborhood crime deterrent.) With the radio off, he'd sit

---

VERSES TO FIGHT BACK FEAR

- **Isaiah 26:3:** You will keep in perfect peace all who trust in you, whose thoughts are fixed on you!
- **Isaiah 41:10:** Don't be afraid, for I am with you. Do not be dismayed, for I am your God. I will strengthen you. I will help you. I will uphold you with my victorious right hand.
- **Isaiah 43:1-2:** Do not be afraid, for I have ransomed you. I have called you by name; you are mine. When you go through deep waters and great trouble, I will be with you. When you go through rivers of difficulty, you will not drown!
- **Matthew 6:31-33:** So don't worry about having enough food or drink or clothing. Why be like the pagans who are so deeply concerned about these things? Your heavenly Father already knows all your needs, and he will give you all you need from day to day if you live for him and make the Kingdom of God your primary concern.
- **John 14:27:** I am leaving you with a gift—peace of mind and heart. And the peace I give isn't like the peace the world gives. So don't be troubled or afraid.
- **Romans 15:13:** So I pray that God, who gives you hope, will keep you happy and full of peace as you believe in him. May you overflow with hope through the power of the Holy Spirit.
- **Philippians 4:6-7:** Don't worry about anything; instead, pray about everything. Tell God what you need, and thank him for all he has done. If you do this, you will experience God's peace, which is far more wonderful than the human mind can understand. His peace will guard your hearts and minds as you live in Christ Jesus.
- **Colossians 3:15:** And let the peace that comes from Christ rule in your hearts. For as members of one body you are all called to live in peace.

---

quietly in the car for a few moments and gather his thoughts. He'd first close his eyes and place his palms facedown on his thighs. Then he'd think back on all the hurtful words, angry thoughts, dishonoring actions, or whatever he'd gone through that might negatively color his evening at home. Then, after praying through and confessing all the "bad" in the day, he'd turn his palms faceup and pray that God would fill his life with love and peace and patience.

> **Wisdom really comes down to fearing the right thing—and the right Person—for the right reasons.**

He'd take that five minutes to "breathe out the bad stuff and breathe in the good," spiritually speaking—and then he'd head home, walking in the door feeling like he'd left the better part of his frustrations in better hands than his own.

That's just what Diane started doing—and it made a huge difference in her home. Out with the bad with palms down—in with the good with palms upraised to a loving God. Try that as a wise way of dealing with pent-up anger, fear, or frustration from a trying day.

CULTIVATING THE RIGHT KIND OF FEAR

We've already seen in Proverbs 29:25 that "fearing people is a dangerous trap." But there is a type of fear that can be tremendously beneficial as you seek to

· · ·

walk in wisdom. That's the fear of the Lord. Just look at how positive the right kind of "fear" is:

- Fear of the Lord is the beginning of wisdom. (Proverbs 9:10)
- Fear of the Lord lengthens one's life. (Proverbs 10:27)
- Those who fear the Lord are secure. (Proverbs 14:26)
- Fear of the Lord is a life-giving fountain. (Proverbs 14:27)
- Fear of the Lord teaches a person to be wise. (Proverbs 15:33)
- Fear of the Lord gives life, security, and protection from harm. (Proverbs 19:23)

Fearing God isn't in the same ballpark as the kind of fear in a Stephen King novel. That kind of fear leads to sleepless nights, not peaceful hearts. Fearing God means looking at who he is and recognizing his power and majesty and depth and uncompromising truth. Like the apostle Peter, we find ourselves falling to our knees before Jesus and saying, "Oh, Lord, please leave me—I'm too much of a sinner to be around you" (Luke 5:8). But it also means looking at God's love, grace, mercy, compassion and counsel and realizing he loves you so much he sacrificed his only Son to ensure your safety and wholeness and to make your relationship with him possible.

Wisdom, then, really comes down to fearing the right thing—and the right Person—for the right reasons.

. . . 7 . . .

HEALTHY HABIT #3: RESISTING TEMPTATION AND OVERCOMING ADDICTIONS

The "instant fix" nature of our modern society leads many people to push every problem or negative feeling aside. Unfortunately, many of these same people try to self-medicate these feelings in negative ways. For example, a woman who has a fight with her husband may go to the mall and buy something to make herself feel better. Or she struggles with her boss, so she stops by the local pub "where everybody knows your name"— and where everyone else hates his boss too—to have a few drinks before going home. Or a man struggles with feeling accepted, so he goes along with "friends" who are doing Ecstasy or smoking marijuana.

All of these reactions carry with them potential for great harm. Certainly there are many Christians who may decide to drink a glass of wine with a meal—moderate consumption of alcohol isn't the issue. But hammering down a few drinks after work can lead to getting drunk and eventually to alcoholism. I have counseled several "serial spenders" who max out credit card after credit card because the only time they feel valuable is when they buy something. Several of these clients lost their homes and marriages as a result!

> Addictions pull us away from wisdom and positive people, and ultimately they can leave us lonely all the time.

And perhaps it's worst of all to push aside moral and legal boundaries to "feel good" at a rave or party or even in private by doing illegal drugs. Crossing the line to do "designer drugs" or marijuana does in fact become the first step to an out-of-control addiction.

Let's take the case of alcohol. For those who drink to excess, just listen to the scathing words of the prophet Isaiah: "Destruction is certain for you who get up early to begin long drinking bouts that last late into the night" (Isaiah 5:11). Looking for happiness or an inflated sense of importance or self, these drinkers are actually bringing down destruction on themselves and their families.

When a new college year starts, we often read

newspaper reports of someone who died in a drinking or initiation party. Here's that word *destruction* again: "Destruction is certain for those who are heroes when it comes to drinking, who boast about all the liquor they can hold" (Isaiah 5:22). Why so much destruction to those whose lives revolve around strong drink? Because alcohol by its very nature is a depressant, not a stimulant. It's chemically formulated to lower inhibitions (hence the buzz or initial warm feelings) even as it continues to lower a person deeper into despair and sadness.

HOW LONELINESS LEADS TO SELFISHNESS

So why do so many people get trapped by strong drink, drugs, or other addictive behaviors? Look at this insight and warning found in the book of Proverbs: "A recluse is self-indulgent, snarling at every sound principle of conduct" (18:1). What does this verse have to do with addictions? In the Scriptures, the word *life* means movement. Guess what the word *death* means? Separation.

The more isolated and cut off you are from others, the more you pull into your own world. And the more consumed you get with your own world, the more you seek to satisfy your own desires or wrap yourself around your own pleasures and the more you leave others—and wisdom—behind.

• • •

That kind of extreme selfishness—driven by an even deeper loneliness—pushes people to wrap their lives around some type of "pleasure intensifier" like cocaine, alcohol, sex, shopping, or gambling. Addictions pull us away from wisdom and positive people, and ultimately they can leave us feeling lonely all the time. Addicted people are indeed headed toward destruction.

The more you wrap yourself in yourself, the lonelier you'll be. The more lonely you are, the more temptation you will face to self-medicate that deep pain with something addictive. Self-absorption leads to death, not life, and thankfully, loneliness doesn't have to be fatal.

TEN WISE WAYS TO BEAT BACK LONELINESS

Relationships are part of God's "way of wisdom"—after all, he created people to need other people. Remember how isolation can lead to dangerous paths of destruction and do your best to make choices that promote close friendships. Here are a few ideas to help you get started.

1. **Start your own "Dinner Club."** Talk to several people at work or at your church about a once-a-month Dinner Club. Take turns picking restaurants or cooking at one another's homes. In the

process of sharing meals, relational bridges can become strong friendships.

2. **Write one note a day.** One cancer survivor we know decided to get her eyes off herself by writing one note a day to someone in her hometown who had lost a loved one. No preaching or "I know how you feel" statements. Just simple handwritten thoughts of love and concern along with a prayer and verse for the family left behind. It was like a note from heaven for many. You don't have to pick only hurting people to minister to with words in a card. But cheering another person's day with a note is a great way to open your world and combat loneliness.

3. **Study Psalm 103.** For those of us whose loneliness goes way back to a parent who was never there for us, God's Word can become a real anchor. Try studying Psalm 103 in depth. It's hard to convince yourself that you're "all alone" when you learn about the dozen ways God shows his love to you.

4. **Pray through your Christmas cards.** Don't just toss your Christmas cards; instead turn them into a prayer basket. For the month after Christmas, and again in July, drag out last year's stack of cards and pray for one family each night. Perhaps even give them a call or drop them a note and let

them know you prayed for them—and thank them for their card!

5. **Pick a school to help.** Did you know that in most towns and cities, there's a school within walking or driving distance that could really use your help? If you feel cut off from other people, try volunteering to read to students who need help, be a lunch monitor, make copies for teachers, or cut out projects. It's tough to stay lonely when you've got a hundred or more students and teachers who need volunteers like you.

6. **Use Thanksgiving as your "thank you" day for your friends.** Your Christmas card might be just one of many a friend receives, so why not be different? Why not send your Christmas card at Thanksgiving—giving thanks for God and for each friend you want to greet. Your card will stand out in an honoring way and may even help build a deeper bond with someone touched by your kind words.

7. **Start a running or exercise group.** Yes, people do get up at 5:30 A.M. to exercise. I see my wife and two friends do it three times a week! What a great way for them to build bonds that can help them when times are tough. I call it their "5K Talk" instead of their "5K Walk."

8. **Develop your musical talent.** Even though you're an adult, it's not too late to learn to sing or play

an instrument—and sometimes the louder the better. I play the bagpipes, which, when played indoors, can cause the dog and my girls to run for cover! Whether it's an "old geezers" band that plays only the oldies, a gospel quartet, the choir at church, or the local orchestra, it's hard to be lonely when you mix people and music.

9. **Adopt the closest sporting venue as your mission field.** Did you know that there is a tremendous mission field every Sunday morning at hundreds of locations across our country? Those are the race tracks where ministries like Pro Racers Outreach and Pro Racers for Christ hold chapels, hand out tracts, pray with racers, and more. Sure it's an outside-the-box way of ministering to others, but it's yet another way to get connected.

10. **Visit the elderly.** There are long-term-care facilities in most communities. And if ever there was a way to get rid of your own feelings of isolation, it's by seeing the faces of people who haven't had a visitor in ten years. When you spend time serving others, you won't have time to focus on your own loneliness.

I hope one of these ideas will work for you—or will spark an idea in your mind of something else you can do to make sure you keep on connecting with others.

HEALTHY HABIT #4: STRENGTHENING YOUR MARRIAGE AND FAMILY

When it comes to gaining wisdom to build a strong marriage, there's a proverb and a practice that can be of significant help. The proverb reads, "Beginning a quarrel is like opening a floodgate, so drop the matter before a dispute breaks out" (Proverbs 17:14). It's put even more pointedly in another proverb, "Avoiding a fight is a mark of honor; only fools insist on quarreling" (Proverbs 20:3). But let's go back to the idea of anger and strife being like "opening a floodgate."

If you've ever been to Arizona, where I live, you might have seen areas in some towns that look like they're flooded in the middle of summer, even though there's been no rain for months. That's because they

. . .

are flooded! People in these homes don't have sprinkler systems in their yards. Instead, the yards have berms that slope up, and twice a month a water-department worker literally floods each yard with water in a controlled manner. That's not the type of flooding pictured here in Proverbs. When anger begins to break out between spouses, it's more like the uncontrolled flooding that costs people their homes, farms, businesses, and more.

STICK TO THE ISSUES

What's a "wise" couple to do? For one thing, make a commitment to keep issues at the issue level.

In the quest to keep disagreements from turning to arguments and eventually to major fights, let me point out a three-step process too many couples choose to make. It begins with some type of issue: save or spend; discipline the kids or be lenient with them; go to the mountains or the beach. We'll call this Level One.

All (honest) couples have disagreements at times. But if a couple can't agree or talk through a particular issue in a positive way, sometimes a spouse will up the ante and begin attacking the other spouse—this is Level Two.

Once each starts attacking the other (perhaps saying things like, "You're such a skinflint." "Oh, yeah?

You're such a spendthrift." "Why don't you become a better steward?" "Why don't you become more submissive?"), they've left behind the actual issue at hand and have moved on to simply hurting each other with their words and actions. If they're not careful, they'll move on to Level Three.

Level Three is when spouses say out loud, or at least to themselves, "If these are the kind of arguments we're going to have, and if you're that kind of person, then what in the world am I doing in this relationship?"

> **If you are married and have a family, your best hope for close support and love and friendship is right there in your household.**

If you're serious about adding wisdom to your marriage, you've got to set your "marriage alert" alarm to stop you at Level Two. When and if you and your spouse get to that attack-and-hurt stage, instantly stop arguing. Find a way to get that disagreement back to Level One, where you are working together on a particular issue. This is the "Get Back to Level One" policy. As soon as you sense that you're attacking, or not listening, or not solving problems, let those Level-Two actions be like bright warning lights on the dashboard. Take a time-out to cool down until you can talk through an issue calmly once again. You don't want to move up this very negative ladder of attacking an issue to attacking a person to attacking your relationship. The fall from the top of this particular ladder can prove fatal to families if left unchecked.

RELATIONSHIP BUILDERS

Remember how destructive isolation can become? If you are married and have a family, your best hope for close support and love and friendship is right there in your household. So those are the relationships to protect and cherish at all costs.

Look for ways to make your spouse and children know they are loved and accepted by you. Pass along your blessing on their lives with your

- appropriate, meaningful touch,
- spoken words,
- communicated hopes and dreams for their special future,
- and genuine commitment.

So let your words of love and encouragement fall on your spouse, and don't fail to pass along a parental blessing to your children as a powerful picture of God's love.

TWO FULL-TIME JOBS

There's a verse in the book of Hebrews that always seems contradictory at first glance. Hebrews 4:11

reads, "Be diligent to enter [God's] rest" (NKJV). Doesn't the idea of being diligent to enter rest sound a bit oxymoronic—like "jumbo shrimp"? Doesn't it seem like two polar extremes are being forced together?

Actually, it's a wise picture of rest, and the same principle can make a marriage or family strong. In Hebrews, God's "rest" can be seen in the way he created the world. For six days he labored; on the seventh day he rested. That idea of working to enter a time of rest isn't contradictory; in fact, it's at the core of any successful business or family.

For example, I'll never forget the freedom that came when I finally realized—several years into my marriage—that I had two full-time jobs. When we were

---

LOOKING FOR THE NEED BEHIND THE DEED

One of the wisest things you can do when another person's actions seem out of place is to ask this question: "What's the need behind that deed?" If your three-year-old falls on the floor in tears, is she being defiant? Perhaps. Or maybe there's an unmet need behind the deed. Is she exhausted because you dragged her all over the mall with no nap or snack? If your teenager comes home and locks himself in his room without even a hello, what's the need behind the deed? Is he being rebellious? Perhaps. Or does he have good reason to believe you're not willing to listen to what's on his heart?

This is a good principle to use with people at work or at church as well. You use your imagination to anticipate others' needs—not to excuse people's sin or wrong behavior but to help you understand how they can do things that seem so out of place. What's the need behind that deed?

first married, I saw home as a place to rest from my real job. What I didn't realize was that Cindy wanted me to come home to relate—and to do the occasional chore as well.

Once you realize that it is *labor first* that brings rest, it totally changes your attitude toward your spouse asking you to do an important errand during the fourth quarter of the football game, toward the kids waking you up at 6:30 A.M. on a Saturday morning to play, or toward your spouse waking you up "just to talk" about something important.

Instead of resenting those requests for interaction or help as intrusions, you can begin to recognize them as opportunities to create closeness—and genuine rest. God's kind of rest comes from a heart that knows it has done the right thing.

> Use your imagination to anticipate others' needs—not to excuse people's sin or wrong behavior but to help you understand how they can do things that seem so out of place.

... 9 ...

HEALTHY HABIT #5:
PUTTING OFF PROCRASTINATION

All through the book of Proverbs, there's a running commentary and contrast between the wise man and the sluggard. An example of a sluggard's actions is found in Proverbs 22:13: "The lazy person is full of excuses, saying, 'If I go outside, I might meet a lion in the street and be killed!' "

Can you see the irony and lack of reality in the sluggard's words? First of all, he's not in the streets. "There's a lion outside," he says, implying he's inside where it's safe. But when was the last time you saw a pride of lions roaming your street? It's his fear, not the actual frightening possibility of coming face-to-face with the king of the jungle, that keeps him from getting out there to work or to mingle. Probability, remote possibility, even the rumor of being hurt in some way—any of these is enough to make him put off any attempt to connect with others.

Fear has a way of pushing people away from others—just like it did for the Roman governor Felix long ago. In the book of Acts, the apostle Paul is brought before Felix—not for another trial, but simply because Felix is curious about his famous prisoner. Paul fearlessly preaches to him three things—righteousness, self-control, and the judgment to come. But "Felix was terrified. 'Go away for now,' he replied. 'When it is more convenient, I'll call for you again'" (Acts 24:25).

PROCRASTINATE THE FEAR AWAY?

Generally there are four types of fear that push people away from making changes in their lives and into procrastination. They are:

- Fear of success
- Fear of failure
- Fear of being controlled
- Fear of intimacy

For the Roman governor Felix, the fear of having to give up control of his life to Christ was most likely what caused him to push Paul away and turn into a spiritual procrastinator.

How about you? The next time you hear a message that convicts you concerning righteousness, self-control, or the judgment to come, see if you don't start pushing back from what's been said. And if you do, then ask yourself, "What am I afraid of?" Are you afraid you'll fail at what's being asked of you? Are you afraid that you'll succeed and the additional expectations will be too much? Perhaps you don't want to let go of an area or attitude in your life. Or maybe you're afraid to let someone really get that close to you.

> Fear has a way of pushing people away from others.

Part of walking in wisdom is being willing to ditch procrastination for action—an action that might require us to face a few fears. Stepping into that way of wisdom is taking a step of faith—faith that God will help and sustain you in whatever you must accomplish.

. . . 10 . . .

THE WONDERFUL WAY OF WISDOM

Remember *The Wonderful World of Disney*? That regular TV program was all make-believe, of course, but you've got something better, something real, to settle on as the foundation of your life choices and actions—the wonderful way of wisdom. God's wisdom is real—and tried and tested by many, many people who have found it to be the "way of life" that leads to joy and the pleasures of living with God (Psalm 16:11).

If you've never put your nose into God's book, the Bible, as a resource for wisdom, consider trying this experiment. You might want to start in the book of Proverbs, a book of wisdom that I've mentioned so often in this little book. Or you might want to dive right into the Gospel of John and read about the greatest example of wise and godly living there ever was: Jesus. But don't hesitate to give it your full attention and a real attempt. I have confidence that you'll find yourself growing in wisdom as you line up your own thinking and ideals with those of the One who created this world we all live in.

> **Throw away the things that hold you back so that you can run the race in freedom and strength.**

Remember Wisdom, the woman calling out from the crossroads with gentle persuasion? She's calling to you—and to me—and to all of us who struggle along with so many decisions to make every day. Listen to her voice!

Remember my marathon, too, and throw away the things that hold you back so that you can run the race in freedom and strength, keeping your eyes on the Savior. There's no better exercise to make you spiritually and emotionally fit!

BOOKS

On Gaining God's Perspective on Life and Decision Making

Bruce and Stan Search for the Meaning of Life by Bruce Bickel and Stan Jantz. A funny and wonderfully readable book for anyone who is struggling with God's reality or presence in the decision-making process.

The Great House of God by Max Lucado. When it comes to living and dying well, Max Lucado's wise counsel on what awaits us in heaven is a faith-stirring book.

The Practical Wisdom of Proverbs by Louis Goldberg. You'll find here a listing of many topics (from finances to fear to anger) and specific Proverbs that relate to these issues.

Reaching for the Invisible God by Philip Yancey. Another thought-provoking, encouraging tool for those who may be doubting the power of prayer or God's ability to help them.

The Useful Proverbs by Kathy Collard Miller. Another good listing of Proverbs by life categories.

On Wisdom for Facing Difficult Times and People

Bold Love by Dan Allender and Tremper Longman, III. A challenging book that can give important insights to readers to make those difficult decisions and deal with difficult people.

Boundaries by Henry Cloud and John Townsend. Another Christian classic that helps people make the wise decision to put up appropriate boundaries against difficult situations and people.

The Control Freak by Les Parrott III, Ph.D. In company with another book he's written, *High-Maintenance Relationships*, this book gives pages of practical insights on dealing with difficult people.

Traveling Mercies: Some Thoughts on Faith by Anne Lamott. These short thoughts on faith and God's love come from a new Christian who is an outstanding writer. While the book contains some objectionable language and challenging content, the personal struggles the author faced in coming to faith, as well as the heartfelt ways she describes both the good and bad decisions she's made, make for inspiring reading.

On Wisdom for Dealing with Emotions and Personal Issues

Feeling Guilty, Finding Grace by Larry K. Weeden. Larry Weeden has edited numerous Gold Medallion books and now has written his own book on turning negative feelings into positive gain.

Healing for Damaged Emotions by David A. Seamands. A classic in dealing with negative emotions like anger, worry, and fear.

Pure Desire by Ted Roberts. A very candid look at the area of sexual temptation and how to make right choices in this important area.

On Wisdom to Help You Become a Loving Spouse, Parent, or Friend

The Complete Financial Guide for Young Couples by Larry Burkett. Larry Burkett is the elder statesman of Christian financial experts and offers sound counsel on making wise financial choices.

■ ■ ■

The Five Love Needs of Men and Women by Gary and Barbara Rosberg. A practical, helpful look at how to build a strong marriage by understanding and meeting your loved one's deepest needs.

The Gift of the Blessing by Gary Smalley and John Trent. Specific help for parents on how to "bless" their child, as well as extensive material on dealing with past hurts and disappointments.

Parents' Guide to the Spiritual Growth of Children by John Trent, Rick Osborne, and Kurt Bruner. For parents looking to "train up a child" in godly ways, this is a hands-on, practical book.

The Second Half of Marriage by David and Claudia Arp. Read by yourself or in a small group, this is an outstanding look at the challenges and opportunities that come to those heading toward empty nests and beyond.

WEB SITES

On Wisdom for Dealing with Finances
www.RonBlue.com
www.DaveRamsey.com
www.crown.org

RADIO PROGRAMS

Insight for Living—Dr. Chuck Swindoll communicates biblical truth and its application to daily life.

Focus on the Family—Dr. James Dobson provides wise counsel on family issues.

Hugh Hewitt Show—Hugh Hewitt challenges people to think wisely about daily events.

. . . ENDNOTES . . .

[1] Pew Internet and American Life Project. 2002–2002.
<www.pewinternet.org>

[2] Norman Nie and Lutz Erbring, *Internet and Society.* The
Stanford Institute for the Quantitative Study of Society.
February 16, 2000. <www.stanford.edu/group/siqss/
Press_Release/internetStudy.html>

[3] E. M. Forster, "The Machine Stops," in *The Collected Tales
of E. M. Forster* (New York: Alfred A. Knopf, 1947), 144.

[4] William Ernest Henley, "Invictus," stanzas 1, 2, and 4.

Marriage Alive International, Inc., founded by husband-wife team Claudia and David Arp, MSW, is a nonprofit marriage- and family-enrichment ministry dedicated to providing resources, seminars, and training to empower churches to help build better marriages and families. The Arps are marriage and family educators, popular speakers, award-winning authors, and frequent contributors to print and broadcast media. They have appeared as marriage experts on programs such as *Today, CBS This Morning,* and *Focus on the Family.* Their Marriage Alive seminar is in great demand across the U.S. and in Europe.

The Mission of Marriage Alive is to identify, train, and empower leaders who invest in others by building strong marriage and family relationships through the integration of biblical truth, contemporary research, practical application, and fun.

Our Resources and Services
- Marriage and family books and small-group resources
- Video-based educational programs including *10 Great Dates to Energize Your Marriage* and *Second Half of Marriage*
- Marriage, pre-marriage, and parenting seminars, including *Before You Say "I Do," Marriage Alive, Second Half of Marriage,* and *Empty Nesting*
- Coaching, mentoring, consulting, training, and leadership development

CONTACT MARRIAGE ALIVE INTERNATIONAL AT WWW.MARRIAGEALIVE.COM OR (888) 690-6667.

The Smalley Relationship Center, founded by Dr. Gary Smalley, offers many varied resources to help people strengthen their marriage and family relationships. The Center provides marriage enrichment products, conferences, training material, articles, and clinical services—all designed to make your most important relationships *successful* relationships.

The Mission of the Smalley Relationship Center is to increase marriage satisfaction and lower the divorce rate by providing a deeper level of care. We want to help couples build strong, successful, and satisfying marriages.

Resources and Services:
- Nationwide conferences: Love Is a Decision, Marriage for a Lifetime
- Counseling services: Couples Intensive program, phone counseling
- Video series, including *Keys to Loving Relationships, Homes of Honor,* and *Secrets to Lasting Love*
- Small group leadership guide
- Articles on marriage, parenting, and stepfamilies
- Smalley Counseling Center provides counseling, national intensives, and more for couples in crisis

CONTACT SMALLEY RELATIONSHIP CENTER AT WWW.SMALLEYONLINE.COM OR 1-800-84-TODAY.